LEARN
TOGETHER
ENGLISH

ENGLISH TESTS

300 questions
to help your child with
PUNCTUATION

Richard Dawson

Macmillan
Children's Books

First published 1996 by Macmillan Children's Books
a division of Macmillan Publishers Limited
25 Eccleston Place, London SW1W 9NF
and Basingstoke

Associated companies throughout the world

ISBN 0 330 34661 X

9 8 7 6 5 4 3 2 1

A CIP catalogue record for this book is available from the British Library.

Typeset by Macmillan Children's Books. Printed by Henry Ling Ltd, The Dorset Press, Dorchester.

Fill in the capital letters, full stops, commas and question marks for these sentences.

the children ran out to play in the snow after putting on their hats coats and boots

_____

_____

the tv programmes were not very good so robert rented a video called robin hood

_____

_____

alan michael david and anne went into the shop and bought crisps apples biscuits and cake for the picnic

_____

_____

france italy spain and portugal are all countries in europe

_____

_____

have you been to spain for your holidays

_____

margaret packed her sun lotion glasses and
newspaper to take down to the beach

_____

_____

the beach looked very peaceful as the sun set over
the golden sea

_____

_____

as the sun rose in the morning the shoreline was
covered with curlew snipe and oystercatchers
feeding on the early-morning worms

_____

_____

_____

wriggle wriggle little worm

_____

in the usa many people have ham eggs and pancakes for breakfast

_____

_____

the dog the cat and the rabbit lived on a farm in yorkshire

_____

_____

numbers 5 22 15 and 7 were amongst the winning numbers of the lottery

_____

_____

oranges lemons and bananas cannot be farmed in this country but apples pears and cherries are grown here

_____

_____

_____

the greengrocer gave his unsold carrots lettuces and cabbages to the rspca to feed their animals

_____

_____

bbc1 bbc2 itv and channel 4 were all showing the fa cup final

_____

_____

do you prefer watching the tv or listening to the radio

_____

_____

do many people go to the usa for their holidays

_____

the fish did not eat the long thin red worms but loved the short fat yellow ones

_____

_____

the jolly pirate sailed to the desert island to bury his sparkling treasure

_____

_____

as we crossed canada by train we saw many animals including moose bears beavers and deer

_____

_____

the ferry carried lorries coaches cars and caravans across the channel to france

_____

_____

the rn captain had commanded an aircraft carrier

_____

the caribbean is made up of many islands including
jamaica barbados grenada and st vincent

_____

_____

the caribbean sea is very warm and teeming with
tropical fish

_____

_____

Note to parents

Each day when your children come home from school you wonder what they have learned. What do children do in English? When do they learn to punctuate? Tests 300 shows the kind of punctuation exercises they should be able to do at the end of year 4 in school. Some of the sentences may be hard for your child. Help them by reading the text out loud and pausing where commas and full stops should go. Enjoy this book with your child, and if your child experiences difficulty with punctuation do not worry but have a quiet word with their teacher.

Each page is illustrated, making the task more interesting and enjoyable. This pull-out centre section gives the answers and guidance on letter formation for you to practise with your child. There is one point for each punctuation mark. You can fill in your child's score at the bottom of this page.

Now fill in your score . . .

Are you at the
top of the tree?

100	200	300
90	190	290
80	180	280
70	170	270
60	160	260
50	150	250
40	140	240
30	130	230
20	120	220
10	110	210

Handwriting advice

It is important that letters are formed correctly. Here is a guide . . . .

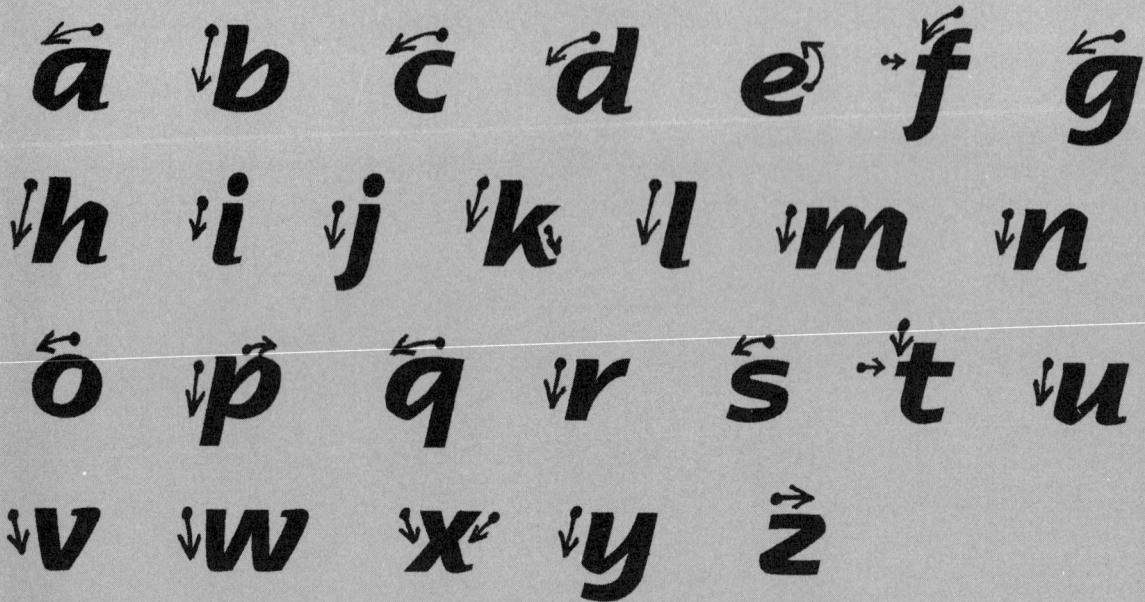

a b c d e f g

h i j k l m n

o p q r s t u

v w x y z

Practise on these.

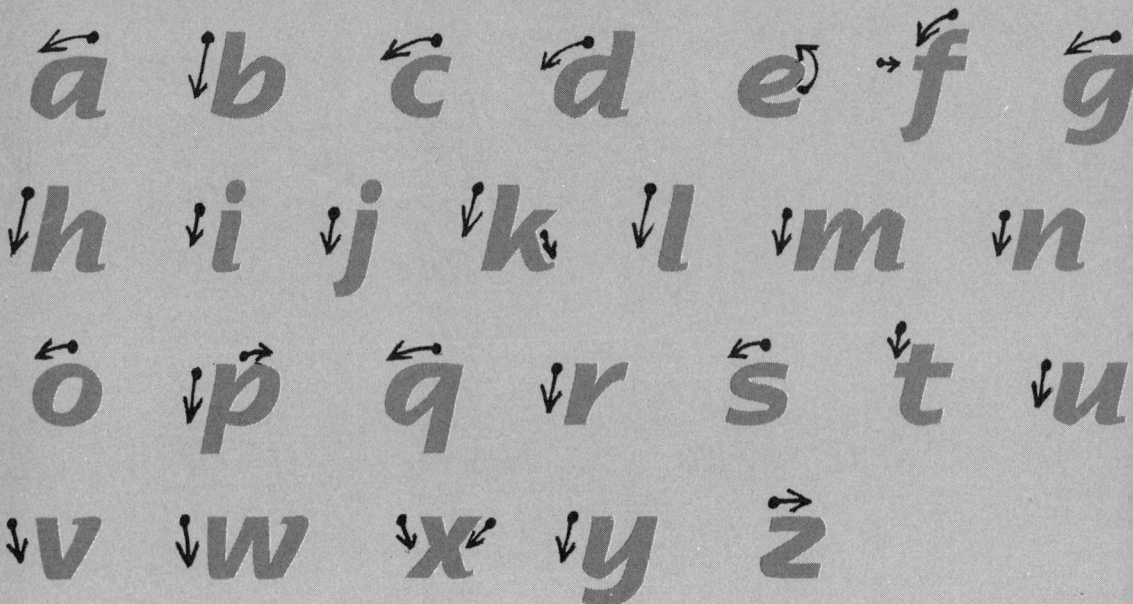

a b c d e f g

h i j k l m n

o p q r s t u

v w x y z

12

Answers

P3
The children ran out to play in the snow after putting on their hats, coats and boots.

The **TV** programmes were not very good so Robert rented a video called Robin Hood.

Alan, Michael, David and Anne went into the shop and bought crisps, apples, biscuits and cake for the picnic.

France, Italy, Spain and Portugal are all countries in Europe.

P4
Have you been to Spain for your holidays?

Margaret packed her sun lotion, glasses and newspaper to take down to the beach.

The beach looked very peaceful as the sun set over the golden sea.

P5
As the sun rose in the morning the shoreline was covered with curlew, snipe and oystercatchers feeding on the early-morning worms.

Wriggle, wriggle, little worm.

P6
In the **USA** many people have ham, eggs and pancakes for breakfast.

The dog, the cat and the rabbit lived on a farm in Yorkshire.

Numbers 5, 22, 15 and 7 were amongst the winning numbers of the lottery.

P7
Oranges, lemons and bananas cannot be farmed in this country but apples, pears and cherries are grown here.

The greengrocer gave his unsold carrots, lettuces and cabbages to the **RSPCA** to feed their animals.

BBC1, **BBC**2, **ITV** and Channel 4 were all showing the **FA** Cup Final.

P8
Do you prefer watching the **TV** or listening to the radio?

Do many people go to the **USA** for their holidays?

The fish did not eat the long, thin, red worms but loved the short, fat, yellow ones.

P9
The jolly pirate sailed to the desert island to bury his sparkling treasure.

As we crossed Canada by train we saw many animals including moose, bears, beavers and deer.

The ferry carried lorries, coaches, cars and caravans across the Channel to France.

P10
The **RN** Captain had commanded an aircraft carrier.

The Caribbean is made up of many islands including Jamaica, Barbados, Grenada and St Vincent.

The Caribbean Sea is very warm and teeming with tropical fish.

P15
In his fish tank James had guppies, angelfish, swordfish and catfish.

The fish and chip shop closed at 1 p.m.

P16
Do you like salt, vinegar and ketchup on your chips?

The small yellow boat sailed quickly across the lake in the **NE** winds.

The race was very exciting. James came first, Paul was second, Edward third.

P17
Did you do maths, English and French at school today?

No, we missed French because Miss Lapin was away.

Have you got maths and English homework?

Answers (continued)

P18

As it flitted from flower to flower the **Red Admiral** butterfly looked very beautiful.

The moon does not shine but reflects the light from the sun.

In 1969 astronauts from the **USA** landed on the moon.

P19

The jungles of **S**outh America contain a wide range of animals including jaguars, tapirs, sloths and a nasty biting fish called the piranha.

Do you know any other animals that have spots?

The cheetah, leopard and jaguar have spots but the tiger has stripes.

P20

Many wild animals are kept in **L**ondon Zoo which is in **R**egent's **P**ark.

What would you like in your sandwich?

Can I have a **BLT**, that is a bacon, lettuce and tomato sandwich.

Today's screening of the feature film 'Gone with the Wind' will be at 3 p.m., 6 p.m. and 9 p.m.

The signs of the zodiac are **A**ries, **T**aurus, **G**emini, **C**ancer, **L**eo, **V**irgo, **L**ibra, **S**corpio, **S**agittarius, **C**apricorn, **A**quarius and **P**isces.

P21

After the snow had melted many places had severe floods.

The valley was filled with swirling, rushing water.

Many bridges were washed away and the village of **N**orth **O**rmsby was flooded.

P22

On the bottom of his party invitation **R**ichard had written **RSVP**.

The bright, yellow football shirts were worn by **N**orwich **C**ity.

On sports day there were many events including the sack race, high jump and obstacle race, and the day ended with a relay.

P23

The **O**lympic Games started in Greece many years ago.

Many of the events like discus, javelin and wrestling were fighting activities.

The countries had competitions instead of making war.

Medals are awarded for prizes in the **O**lympic Games; gold for first, silver for second and bronze for third.

P24

What did you have for dinner today?

Lucy did not enjoy her school dinner as it was potatoes, cabbage, gravy and cheese pie.

The **H**umberston **F**un **R**un was won by a duck; in second place was **S**uperman and **K**ing **H**enry VIII came third.

Can **I** have a ham sandwich, a salad and some crisps, please?

in his fish tank james had guppies angelfish swordfish and catfish

_____

_____

the fish and chip shop closed at 1 pm

_____

_____

do you like salt vinegar and ketchup on your chips

_____

the small yellow boat sailed quickly across the lake in the ne winds

_____

_____

the race was very exciting james came first paul was second edward third

_____

_____

did you do maths english and french at school today

_____

_____

no we missed french because miss lapin was away

_____

have you got maths and english homework

_____

as it flitted from flower to flower the red admiral butterfly looked very beautiful

_____

_____

the moon does not shine but reflects the light from the sun

_____

_____

in 1969 astronauts from the usa landed on the moon

_____

_____

the jungles of south america contain a wide range of
animals including jaguars tapirs sloths and a nasty
biting fish called the piranha

_____

_____

_____

do you know any other animals that have spots

_____

the cheetah leopard and jaguar have spots but the
tiger has stripes

_____

_____

many wild animals are kept in london zoo which is in regent's park

_____

_____

what would you like in your sandwich

_____

can i have a blt, that is a bacon lettuce and tomato

_____

today's screenings of the feature film 'gone with the wind' will be at 3 pm 6 pm and 9 pm

_____

_____

the signs of the zodiac are aries taurus gemini cancer leo virgo libra scorpio sagittarius capricorn aquarius and pisces

_____

_____

_____

after the snow had melted many places had severe
floods

_____

_____

the valley was filled with swirling rushing water

_____

many bridges were washed away and the village of
north ormsby was flooded

_____

_____

on the bottom of his party invitation richard had written rsvp

_____

_____

the bright yellow football shirts were worn by norwich city

_____

_____

on sports day there were many events including the sack race high jump and obstacle race and the day ended with a relay

_____

_____

_____

the olympic games started in greece many years ago

_____

_____

many of the events like discus javelin and wrestling were fighting activities

_____

_____

the countries had competitions instead of making war

_____

_____

medals are awarded for prizes in the olympic games; gold for first silver for second and bronze for third

_____

_____

_____

what did you have for dinner today

_____

lucy did not enjoy her school dinner as it was
potatoes cabbage gravy and cheese pie

_____

_____

the humberston fun run was won by a duck; in
second place was superman and king henry VIII
came third

_____

_____

_____

can i have a ham sandwich a salad and some crisps
please

_____

_____